GERONIMO

THE REST OF THE STORY

William Howard Heydorn, MD

WestBow Press books may be ordered through booksellers or by contacting:

WestBow Press
A Division of Thomas Nelson & Zondervan
1663 Liberty Drive
Bloomington, IN 47403
www.westbowpress.com
844-714-3454

ISBN: 978-1-6642-7241-5 (sc)
ISBN: 978-1-6642-7243-9 (hc)
ISBN: 978-1-6642-7242-2 (e)

Library of Congress Control Number: 2022913098

Print information available on the last page.

WestBow Press rev. date: 02/01/2023

WESTBOW
P R E S S®
A DIVISION OF THOMAS NELSON
& ZONDERVAN

Contents

Preface v

Chapter 1: The Jumpers 1

Chapter 2: In the Beginning 6

Chapter 3: The Only Good Spaniard/Mexican Is a Dead One: The Indian View of the Situation 9

Chapter 4: The Only Good White Man Is a Dead One: The Indian Has a New Enemy 12

Chapter 5: Geronimo Finds a Hero 16

Chapter 6: Some Things Never Change 19

Chapter 7: Native Americans Learn the Tricks of the Trade 22

Chapter 8: The Missionaries 27

Chapter 9: The Controversy Continues 49

Appendix 1: Correspondence between Howard and Abbie 54

Appendix 2: Howard's Poem to Abbie 64

Preface

The Merriam-Webster Dictionary defines an apologist as "one who speaks or writes in defense of someone or something."[1] In preparation for this book, I read, scanned, or viewed the seemingly endless roots and branches extending from the tree I often refer to as Geronimo, and found that, over eleven decades after his death, he continues to be featured in the news.

Many publications and films describe Geronimo in a favorable light and concentrate on the victimization of Native Americans, whereas others portray Geronimo as a vicious murderer who should have been executed for crimes against society. Some authors have attempted to remain neutral and claim that Geronimo was a complex human being who displayed paranoia and a contradictory personality. With so many books, articles, and films already available on library shelves, a potential reader may ask, "Why another book?" I have three reasons why another book is necessary to tell the rest of the story.

The first is that my grandfather knew Geronimo, having spent time with him during the last eleven years of the iconic Indian's life. Furbeck family lore provides information and photographs from family albums that have never been available to the general public.

Second is that public broadcasting on the West Coast offered a new film series, *Country Music*, by Ken Burns, in the fall of 2019. This is music that is easy to listen to, memorable, and reflects the culture and traditions of the listeners. I was inspired to make frequent references to this music of the people to underscore historical events covered in the narrative.

---

[1] "Apologist," Merriam-Webster.com, accessed October 12, 2021, https://www.merriam-webster.com/dictionary/apologist.

Third is the recognition that although I never met my grandfather, I have come to know and admire him. Howard Rutsen Furbeck was a minister and missionary who was assigned by the Reformed Church in America (commonly referred to as the Dutch Reformed Church) to the mission field in the vicinity of Fort Sill, Oklahoma. It was he who provided the inspiration for this unique tale that tells the rest of the story. No apologies will be offered.

The name, "Geronimo", has been familiar to children and adults throughout the world. It continues to be heard on occasion coming from the diving boards in swimming pools, the high bars in playgrounds, and even in bedrooms. A *Calvin and Hobbes* cartoon depicts Calvin shouting "GERONIMO" as he jumps out of his bedroom window with a sheet for a parachute as his pet observes.

CALVIN AND HOBBES © 1986 Watterson. Reprinted with permission of
ANDREWS MCMEEL SYNDICATION. All rights reserved.

During the 1940s, boys of Kinderhook in upstate New York assumed spring had arrived when ice had melted in the creek that ran through the village. We were ready to test the cold and fast-moving stream. As we jumped off the bridge that spanned the water, we bolstered our courage by shouting "Geronimo."

Martin Van Buren
National Archives (111-B-4142)

Kinderhook was a great place to grow up; it provided an opportunity to attend both the school that bore the name of our eighth president, Martin Van Buren, and attend Kinderhook Dutch Reformed Church, where he had been a member. Van Buren was born, raised, and buried in Kinderhook. Locals knew him as "Old Kinderhook," and if events met the approval of Old Kinderhook, we knew they were OK. OK has been described as the most frequently spoken and written word on the planet, and will be used many times in the narrative, OK?

In late July, we would return to the creek, grasp the vines that extended from the trees that lined the bank, bring them up to the shore, and use them to swing over the slower moving water before dropping into the creek. Again, we always cried "Geronimo!" as we emulated our heroes, who were members of the elite airborne troops. We knew that the water would soon turn brown and bubbly, as the lazy summer stream could no longer clear the effluent from the mills located about two miles to the north. Although environmental waste and water pollution were not part of our vocabulary, when we saw it, we could recognize it.

These days, Marco Polo has replaced Geronimo at the local swimming pool. One suspects the current generation knows no more about Marco Polo than they do about Geronimo.

Chapter 1:

The Jumpers

The concept of jumping out of airplanes as a way to deploy infantry was introduced to the United States Army during World War II.[2] During the summer of 1940, a Parachute Test Platoon was formed to develop techniques to train the parachute units that would follow. The Platoon consisted of forty-eight volunteers, handpicked from a much larger group by a panel of officers.[3]

In Fort Benning, Georgia, the weather was hot, the training arduous, and becoming one of these Goliaths was now a goal for many of the already tough infantry men. After completing several weeks of training and beginning to jump out of airplanes, this select group were known and respected by everyone at Fort Benning. They had become what every soldier wanted to be. Six-foot-eight Private Aubrey Eberhard was the biggest paratrooper in the platoon, and hard work on a farm in rural Georgia had been his prep school. One evening, after a full day of training, Aubrey and three other jumpers took the short walk from their airfield camp to the main post theater to watch a film about an Indian known as Geronimo.

Aubrey would have identified with this Apache warrior. As a child, Geronimo underwent rigorous physical training. A regular challenge was a "long, fast run over rough terrain, usually up a steep slope and back down. To demonstrate that he had done his breathing through his nose, he carried a small stone in his mouth and showed it to mentor on return."[4] Training was supervised by a stern, relentless leader who would have excelled

---

[2] Jay A. Graybeal, "The First U.S. Army Airborne Operation," U.S. Army, posted June 7, 2016, https://www.army.mil/article/3852/the_first_u_s_army_airborne_operation.
[3] Gerard M. Devlin, *Paratrooper!* (New York: St. Martin's Press, 1979), 51.
[4] Robert M. Utley, *Geronimo* (New Haven and London: Yale University Press, 2012), 12.

as an army drill instructor, a superior warrior who convinced these young boys that this was not play but would someday be a matter of life or death. The young men soon realized that these were not games. They were survival techniques, and someday, lives would depend on them.

On the way back to their tents, the men discussed the first mass jump that was planned for the next day. This jump carried more risk that the individual jumps they had already made. Eberhart, with the movie hero still on his mind, informed them that he would remain cool and shout "Geronimo!" The platoon bought the concept, and the next day this unsanctioned yell echoed through the sky.[5]

A few weeks later, visiting dignitaries and senior Washington brass came to observe a jump by the trainees. Some opined that this unfamiliar shout in the middle of a serious activity was a breach of discipline and should be discontinued. However, one senior officer felt the call displayed bravery and managed to convince the other officers that it was effective.[6] The wisdom displayed by this senior officer resulted in "Geronimo" becoming an iconic symbol and cry for individuals facing imminent danger. Two months after the Parachute Test Platoon was formed, the US Army's first airborne tactical unit was activated—the 501st Parachute Infantry Battalion.[7] The battalion grew into regiments, and finally into five airborne divisions. Chief Geronimo's name appeared on caps, lapels, and shirt pockets.

501st PIR "Geronimo" Patch
Photograph by Peter McIntosh, used with permission.

---

[5] Devlin, *Paratrooper!*, 68. In a footnote on page 673, Devlin notes that this information was obtained in a June 1973 interview with Aubrey Eberhart at his home in Roberts, Georgia.
[6] Ed Howard, "Paramount's 1939 western GERONIMO…a forgotten movie with a giant legacy," posted on The Old Corral in September 2004, https://www.b-westerns.com/geronimo.htm.
[7] William B. Breuer, *Geronimo! American Paratroopers in World War II* (New York: St. Martin's Press, 1989), 6.

In September 1943, American jumpers were deployed to England to join Allied troops as they prepared to fly over the English Channel and establish a beachhead in Normandy.[8] On the eve of the D-Day invasion, paratroopers wore war paint and displayed Mohawk haircuts.

Private Ware Applies Last Second Make-up to Private Plaudo in England
National Archives (111-SC-193551)

---

[8] "101st Airborne Division," U.S. Army Center of Military History, accessed October 10, 2021, https://history.army.mil/html/forcestruc/cbtchron/cc/101abd.htm.

Lieutenant Colonel Byron Paige of the 11ᵗʰ Airborne Division wrote a classic World War II paratrooper song that memorialized the event.[9]

> Down from Heaven comes ELEVEN
>
> And there's HELL to pay below
>
> shout "GERONIMO" "GERONIMO"
>
> Hit the silk and check your canopy
>
> and take a look around
>
> The air is full of troopers
>
> set for battle on the ground
>
> Till we join the stick of ANGELS
>
> killed on Leyte and Luzon
>
> shout "GERONIMO" "GERONIMO"
>
> It's a gory road to glory
>
> but we're ready here we go
>
> shout "GERONIMO" "GERONIMO."

"Geronimo" continues to be associated with paratroopers. Over four decades later, William B. Breuer used *Geronimo!* as the title of his book celebrating the fiftieth anniversary of American paratroopers in World War II. The former headquarters of 501ˢᵗ Parachute Infantry Regiment "Klondike" (the code name for the 501ˢᵗ) was located in Veghel in the southern Netherlands. The unit's crest, with the name Geronimo on it, has been displayed in front of the building.

---

[9] Howard, "Paramount's 1939 western GERONIMO."

Former headquarters of 501st Parachute Infantry Regiment
Photograph by E. v.d. Boogaard, taken 14 September 2014 and reprinted without changes
under the Creative Commons Attribution Share Alike 4.0 International license.

After World War II, it was determined that "Geronimo" was never approved in any official training manuals and if called in combat could be a potential bullet magnet. It was not to be heard again in the big sky. Yet troopers of the 501st Parachute Infantry Regiment (PIR) still wear the troop insignia with Geronimo's name, and "Down from Heaven" continues to be played during major ceremonies of the 82nd Airborne.[10]

One wonders if Geronimo listens. He would have been proud to hear it, and Martin Van Buren would have said, "OK."

---

[10] Howard, "Paramount's 1939 western GERONIMO."

Chapter 2:

IN THE BEGINNING

In order to understand the mindset of Geronimo, one must attempt to comprehend the world he was brought into. Geronimo was a member of the Bedonkohe band of the Chiricahua Apache tribe.[11] His Apache name was Goyaałé (meaning "one who yawns"; often spelled Goyathlay or Goyahkla when using an English alphabet.)[12] It is said that during the heat of a bloody conflict with Mexican soldiers, the soldiers were heard to call for mercy from St. Jerome, and after that Goyaałé became known as Geronimo (Spanish for Jerome). Others argue that it was simply a Mexican nickname or a mispronunciation of "Goyahkla".[13]

Geronimo could recall the place of his birth, which was considered sacred. While Geronimo stated that he was born in Arizona,[14] historians place the location as New Mexico.[15] In the 1820s, appellations such as Arizona or New Mexico had not been established; what the white men would eventually name the ground was not relevant to Geronimo. As Chiricahua Apache, a cradle ceremony would have been performed four days after birth.[16] In the ceremony, the newborn Indian is marked with pollen, a cradleboard is presented to the four directions, and then the child is placed into the cradleboard.

---

[11] Utley, *Geronimo*, 6.

[12] "Geronimo", accessed October 18, 2021, https://www.webpages.uidaho.edu/~rfrey/329geronimo.htm.

[13] Evan Andrews, "7 Things You May Not Know About Geronimo," History Stories, last modified September 1, 2018, https://www.history.com/news/7-things-you-may-not-know-about-geronimo.

[14] Barrett, *Geronimo's Story of His Life* (New York: Duffield & Company, 1906), 17.

[15] Utley, *Geronimo*, 12.

[16] "Some Apache Ceremonies," March 10, 2017, http://nativeamericannetroots.net/diary/2277.

When he was seventeen, Geronimo was admitted to the "council of the warriors."[17] He was made a war chief in 1859 after going to battle to avenge the death of his wife and children, which had occurred a year earlier.[18]

Many sources report that Geronimo had received a revelation that no bullet or other projectile would kill him.[19] This vision proved to be accurate. At the time of his death, his body contained multiple wounds—none of which were the cause of his death.

The *Merriam-Webster Dictionary* defines genocide as "the deliberate and systematic destruction of a racial, political, or cultural group."[20] Although the word "genocide" was not part of Geronimo's vocabulary, conflict and warfare, including disputes over limited resources, such as prey and water, are virtually ubiquitous features of hunter-gatherer societies. The dictionary also defines the word "covet" as "an inordinate desire for what belongs to another."[21] These flaws in our minds continue to plague the world as we know it, and there is no evidence that this will ever change. Table 1 provides the reader with a small sample of events that meet the modern definition of genocide.

Table 1

God ordains the death of Egyptian firstborn males.	1300 BC
Roman leader Cato declares the destruction of Carthage.	149–146 BC
Nero attempts to eliminate the Christians of Rome.	AD 64
Nazi Germany carries out the Holocaust.	1940s

Expectations of white settlers were very different from those of the Native Americans. Some of those differences are well described in popular songs. Two of the most prolific songwriters of the first half of the nineteenth century were Albert Brumley and Stuart Hamlin. They came from different backgrounds, but both wrote songs that graphically expressed those expectations.

Alfred Brumley was the son of a sharecropper family. He was raised in a religious and musical environment, attended singing school, and attended the Hartford Musical Institute in 1926. He wrote over six hundred

---

17 Barrett, *Geronimo's Story of His Life*, 37.

18 Barrett, *Geronimo's Story of His Life*, 54.

19 Utley, *Geronimo*, 21.

20 "Genocide," Merriam-Webster.com, accessed October 13, 2021, https://www.merriam-webster.com/dictionary/genocide.

21 "Covet," Merriam-Webster.com, accessed October 14, 2021, https://www.merriam-webster.com/dictionary/covet.

songs and has been referred to as "the Dean of Gospel Songwriters."[22] One of his songs, which has been recorded by many artists, provides a vivid musical description of those cultural differences.

> This world is not my home, I'm just a-passing through;
>
> My treasures are laid up somewhere beyond the blue;
>
> The angels beckon me from Heaven's open door,
>
> And I can't feel at home in this world anymore.[23]

Stuart Hamblin was born in 1908 in Texas. His career as an entertainer began in 1931. Not only was he a singing cowboy and composer, he also appeared as an actor in motion pictures with Gene Autry, Roy Rogers, and John Wayne. After years of drinking and gambling, he underwent a religious conversion at a Billy Graham crusade. He was fired from his radio show for refusing to do commercials for alcoholic beverages and became a major supporter of the temperance movement. He ran for president as the Prohibition Party candidate in 1952. His composition "This Old House" tells his audience that he no longer has need for his physical body and is ready to leave this world.[24]

America's settlers had no problem with moving on and giving up their land. Their final destination was unworldly.

[22] Guy Logsdan, "Brumley, Albert Edward (1905-1907," Oklahoma Historical Society, accessed October 25, 2021, https://www.okhistory.org/publications/enc/entry.php?entry=BR027.

[23] Albert E. Brumley, *This World Is Not My Home (I'm Just Passing Thru)*. © Arr. Copyright 1936. Renewed 1964 by Albert E. Brumley & Sons/SESAC (admin. By ClearBox Rights). All rights reserved. Used by permission.

[24] "Stuart Hamblin," accessed August 6, 2022, https://en.wikipedia.org/wiki/Stuart_Hamlin

Chapter 3:

The Only Good Spaniard/Mexican Is a Dead One: The Indian View of the Situation

In the early 1800s, Zebulon Pike, a US Army officer, was deployed to investigate Spanish settlements in New Spain (modern New Mexico), resulting in a trespass of Native American territory. On his second expedition in November 1806, he attempted to climb the peak that now carries his name; however, he was forced to give up due to heavy snow.

Zebulon Pike
Portrait by Charles Wilson Peal, 1808.
This work is in the public domain (Courtesy of Wikimedia Commons)

The small contingent of the US Army was stopped by Spanish officials, charged with illegal entry, escorted to Santa Fe, and finally to Chihuahua where they met Native American Indians. Pike had no bone to pick with the Indians. His stated goal was to "smoke the pipe of peace, bury the tomahawk, and become one nation."[25] Pike envisioned an alliance with the local Native Americans to exterminate (commit genocide against) Spaniards who had come all the way from Europe to intrude on land that was not rightfully theirs.

Picture Geronimo as a young boy sitting near the evening campfire as the elders spoke of times gone by. He may have heard tales of Pike, the US Army, and the Apache, how they had made a good team, and worked together to cleanse the environment of trespassers.

Geronimo was brought up to believe that when Usen (God) created the Apache, He also created their homes in the west. He gave to them such grain, fruits, and game as they needed to eat and to restore their health when afflicted by disease. Usen had created many different herbs, and taught the Apache where to find them and how to prepare them for medicinal use. He gave them a pleasant climate, and all they needed for clothing and shelter was at hand. Geronimo was said to recall, "During my minority we had never seen a missionary or priest. We had never seen a white man and thus quietly lived the Be-don-ko-he Apaches."[26] What more could one ask for? This sheltered life was short-lived.

In 1810, land that had been claimed by the Spanish, after defeating inhabitants who had lived there for centuries, was now to be claimed by a newly independent state of Mexico. Father Hidalgo y Costilla incited the Mexicans to take up war against the Spaniards and any others that prevented freedom for Mexico. The war culminated in 1821 after the Treaty of Cordoba declared Mexico an independent constitutional monarchy. The Mexican approach was very different than that of Pike. No peace pipe was offered. The Mexicans considered the land to legally belong to them, and their goal was to ensure that all but the Mexicans were kept off any desirable patch of land. One way to accomplish this would be to exterminate (genocide) the Apache. Bounties were offered for Indian scalps.[27]

---

[25] Zebulon Pike Quotes, BrainyQuote, accessed May 28, 2022, https://www.brainyquote.com/quotes/zebulon_pike_349687.

[26] Barrett, *Geronimo's Story of His Life,* 34.

[27] Dean Chavers, "Scalping in America," posted on Indian Country Today, updated September 13, 2018, https://indiancountrytoday.com/archive/scalping-in-america.

In his book, *I Fought with Geronimo*, Jason Betzinez (a cousin of Geronimo's) describes the 1850 entrapment and massacre Apache families who had camped along a river near the town of Ramos in northern Chihuahua.[28] The Apache had not realized that the governor of Chihuahua had set a bounty on their heads. When a runner came through the camps inviting everyone to town to drink, Betzinez reports that most of the tribe, "except for the people too old or too young to walk,"[29] accepted the invitation.

The next day, just before the first light, Betzinez describes how soldiers from Mexico slipped into the camp: "In a short time most of the Indians were lying in their blood, dead or dying. The Mexicans fell to work with sharp knives, wrenching off the gory trophies for which they would receive gold and silver from their authorities. It was said that two hundred pesos was the price paid for the scalp of a man, with lesser amounts for those of women and children."[30] Among the dead were Geronimo's wife, mother, and three children.[31]

Betzinez reports that the hospitality shown by the people of Ramos was eventually returned by a band of warriors that included Cochise, Mangas Colorado, Benito, Geronimo, and Tudeevia (Betzinez' grandfather). According to Betzinez, "The men who took part in this battle, especially those who were my kinsmen, later told me that everyone agreed that this was the greatest of Apache victories."[32]

---

[28] Jason Betzinez, *I Fought with Geronimo*, (New York: Bonanza Books, a division of Crown Publishers, Inc., by arrangement with Stackpole Books), 3 and 17. Betzinez appears to have described this incident twice, once in 1850 (p.3) and once in 1858 (p. 17). Readers are alerted that calendars were not generally used by the tribe at the time and some dates are approximations.
[29] Betzinez, *I Fought with Geronimo*, 3.
[30] Betzinez, *I Fought with Geronimo*, 3
[31] Robert Utley, in his biography of Geronimo, reports that Geronimo's family was killed in this incident but places the date as March 5, 1851 (Utley, *Geronimo*, 27).
[32] Betzinez, *I Fought with Geronimo*, p. 8

Chapter 4:

The Only Good White Man Is a Dead One: The Indian Has a New Enemy

President Andrew Jackson
Portrait by Ralph E. W. Earl ca 1835
This work is in the public domain (Courtesy of Wikimedia Commons)

The election of Andrew Jackson in 1829 marked the beginning of the end for Native Americans, although at the time they were not aware of it. The Indian Removal Act of 1830 was established under his presidency, which ran until 1837.

The Act, which was signed into law on May 28, 1830, dispatched North American Indians to land west of the Mississippi, forcing them to leave behind all of their possessions including property, homes, and schools.[33] Under the Act, more than 46,000 Native Americans were forced to abandon their ancestral lands and relocate to Indian Territory, in what is now Oklahoma, in a migration known as the Trail of Tears. The Cherokee were the largest contingent. More than 4,000 Cherokee are believed to have died during their migration in 1838-1839.[34] The Cherokee experience was the first of many displacements. There was no longer sufficient territory to support Native American tribes, which had been promised their land for posterity, and new arrivals.

Although Native American tribes had been at war with immigrants from Europe since as early as 1622,[35] the "Apache Attacks" of 1861–1900 was the war that affected Geronimo most. The attacks started with what came to be known as the Bascom affair.[36]

In January 1861, the Tonto Apache (one of a group of Western Apache) raided the camp of a rancher, stole livestock, and kidnapped the rancher's twelve-year-old stepson, Felix Ward.[37] The incident was reported to a nearby military authority, and Lt. George Nicolas Bascom was directed to recover the boy. Having been told the kidnappers had gone east toward the Chiricahua Mountains, the military wrongly assumed the Chiricahua Apache were responsible. They arranged to meet with Cochise for a discussion of the situation. Cochise assumed this was to be a friendly meeting about a common enemy and came with his brother, two nephews, wife, and two children. Bascom came with over fifty soldiers. To the surprise of Cochise, Bascom arrested the small Indian contingent and refused to release them. The wily Cochise slashed the tent in which he was being held and escaped.

---

[33] "Indian Removal Act," Wikipedia, accessed December 3, 2019, https://en.wikipedia.org/wiki/Indian_Removal_Act.

[34] "May 28, 1830 CE: Indian Removal Act," National Geographic Society, accessed October 17, 2021, https://www.nationalgeographic.org/thisday/may28/indian-removal-act/.

[35] "Indian Wars Time Table," accessed October 10, 2021, https://www.u-s-history.com/pages/h1008.html.

[36] Detailed accounts of the Bascom affair are recorded in *In the Days of Victorio: Recollections of a Warm Springs Apache* by Eve Ball and *A Boy Once Named Felix* by Karen Weston Gonzales.

[37] "Bascom affair," Wikipedia, accessed October 18, 2021, https://en.wikipedia.org/wiki/Bascom_affair.

The Apache felt it only fair to play by the white man's rules, and captured Anglos to exchange for the Cochise family. Ultimately, hostages on both sides were killed. Cochise transferred his hatred of the Mexicans to the white men and, as far as he was concerned, the only good white man would be a dead one.

After ten years of attacks on white settlers and military, Cochise was convinced the cause was futile and it was time to make a treaty. In 1872, after being promised a huge tract of land in southeastern Arizona, he stated, "The white man and Indian are to drink of the same waters, eat of the same bread and be at peace."[38] Two years later, he died of probable stomach cancer.

The family of Cochise did not live to see the bust of Cochise that is now displayed at Fort Bowie National Historic Site. They did live to see the treaty broken and their eventual displacement from the land they believed had been promised to them.

Bronze Bust of Cochise at Fort Bowie National Historic Site
Photo by Mr. Andre Kozimor, used with permission.

Geronimo remained a hold-out. He was not yet ready to give up, although the outcome was inevitable. In 1877, Geronimo and his people were removed to a reservation in San Carlos, Arizona, where they had neither horses nor guns. Geronimo found life on the reservation intolerable. In 1881 Geronimo, with other tribe members, found a way to escape the reservation. They lived freely until 1884 when, weary of continual harassment, they returned to the reservation, much on their own terms. Geronimo's stay did not last long, and Geronimo left again in 1884 with a small contingent. General George Crook was assigned to trap them. [39]

---

[38] History.com Editors, "Cochise," updated March 3, 2022, https://www.history.com/topics/native-a.merican-history/cochise.
[39] History.com Editors, "Apache leader Geronimo flees Ariona reservation, setting off panic," updated September 20, 2021, https://www.history.com/this-day-in-history/geronimo-flees-arizona-reservation.

In his autobiography, Geronimo is critical of General Crook. In this case, Geronimo misunderstood the real General Crook. Many consider Crook to be the army's greatest Indian fighter, however, unlike most of his contemporaries, he respected Native Americans as valiant foes who deserved to be treated fairly in defeat. During the final years of his career, Crook continued his lifelong campaign in favor of his former enemies, speaking out against white encroachments on Indian land, unfair treaties, and failed federal policies. This approach was not looked on favorably by his superiors and, as a result, he was relieved of his command and replaced by General Nelson Miles, whose goal was to rid the west of the Native American Indians (genocide).

The next decade was one of imprisonment, separation, and exile for not only the tribe but the Apache collaborators at US Army installations in Florida and Alabama. In 1894, the survivors and descendants of the Chiricahua Apache tribe, including Geronimo, whose original territory covered much of what is now the American southwest, including eastern Arizona and western Mexico, were permanently relocated to southwestern Oklahoma.

Chapter 5:

Geronimo Finds a Hero

General O. O. Howard
National Archives (111-B-1806)

Geronimo had little good to say about the Army officers with whom he had skirmished for all those many years. The single exception was Oliver Otis Howard. General O.O. Howard had been sent by President Grant in 1872 to make peace with the Apache and meet with Geronimo.

In his autobiography, Geronimo describes the treaty he made with General Howard.

> This treaty lasted until long after General Howard had left our country. He always kept his word with us and treated us as brothers. We never had so good a friend among the United States officers as General Howard. We could have lived forever at peace with him, and even to this day frequently talk of the happy times when General Howard was in command of our Post. After he went away, he placed an agent at Apache Pass who issued to us from the Government clothing, rations, and supplies as General Howard directed. When beef was issued to the Indians I got twelve steers for my tribe, and Cochise got twelve steers for his tribe. Rations were issued about once a month, but if we ran out, we only had to ask and we were supplied. Now, as prisoners of war in this Reservation, we do not get such good rations.[40]

Howard was recognized as the "Christian General" and, as such, was looked upon derisively and with disdain by most of his fellow officers. He was a unique figure in the Civil War.

After graduating from West Point, fourth of forty-six cadets, General Howard fought against the Florida Seminole Indians in 1857. His conversion to evangelical Christianity inspired him to consider becoming a minister. He resisted the call and went on to become a success in the Union and United States armies.

In 1861, his performance as a Brigade Commander at Bull Run earned Howard a promotion to Brigadier General. Misfortune struck, and he lost his right arm a year later at the Battle of Seven Pines (also known as the Battle of Fair Oaks). He was awarded the Medal of Honor and eventually attained the rank of major general. In 1867, he founded Howard University in Washington, DC. General Howard was the president of Howard University from 1869 until 1874[41].

---

[40] Barrett, *Geronimo's Story of His Life*, 128.
[41] "Oliver Otis Howard," accessed May 30, 2022, https://en.wikipedia.org/wiki/Oliver_Otis_Howard.

Howard University is a private, coeducational, nonsectarian, historically Black university. The University remains committed to the education and advancement of underrepresented populations. One may speculate as to how many people are aware that Howard University owes its existence to a white Union Army officer.

Gordon L. Weil's *The Good Man: The Civil War's "Christian General" and his Fight for Racial Equality* tells the story of the general that Geronimo trusted and considered a friend. General Howard and Geronimo both died in 1909.

Chapter 6:

SOME THINGS NEVER CHANGE

It appears that whoever first said "some things never change" may have been right. It has been true as far as it may apply to Native Americans.

Jackson's Indian Removal Act, the emigration of Europeans to North America, and the direction of journalists such as Horace Greeley for young men to "Go West" resulted in the displacement of innumerable Native Americans and multiple attempts to either exterminate them or remake them.

Between the 1800s and the 1850s, thousands of immigrants came to the United States, mostly from Europe. They were predominantly men who came sharing steerage with the rats on dirty, small decks. Europe was overcrowded and crop failures, unemployment, and a chaotic religious and political climate made the situation untenable for many. They believed they would find freedom and plentiful land in a world that would be new to them. It never occurred to the immigrants that the land they sought was already occupied. True Native Americans were and are the indigenous population whose ancestry may go back some 20,000 years.

Many living in the United States may recall singing along with Peter, Paul, and Mary, or perhaps Pete Seeger, claiming that "This Land Is Your Land." The song appealed to a variety of races, political groups, and economic classes. It has also been the subject of controversy. The next time you hear it you might ask yourself, *Why did God take this land from the Native Americans and give it to you and me?*

The quest for gold in California resulted in the California state government passing the Act for Government and Protection of Indians that did anything *but* protect Indians. In fact, it "allowed White Californians to forcibly remove Native Californians from their lands and into indentured servitude."[42] California's first governor, Peter H. Burnett, proclaimed that "a war of extermination will continue to be waged between the two races until the Indian race becomes extinct."[43] The three decades between 1850 and 1880 became known as the time of the California Indian Wars.

Geronimo too was at war. He became a prisoner of war, and was sent to the Mount Vernon Barracks in Alabama with other members of his tribe, including women and children. In his 1916 book, *Famous Indian Chiefs I Have Known*, O.O. Howard reported that, during an interview conducted by an interpreter, Geronimo confided that he had become a school superintendent: "We have fine lady teachers. All the children go to their school. I make them. I want them to be white children."[44]

From among the Indians at Mount Vernon Barracks, two companies of soldiers, each of fifty Indians, were formed. Geronimo claimed to be very proud of them, saying, "Heap big! Tatâh; heap good!" and he told them to do their best to keep their uniforms clean, make their gun barrels shine, and never have dust on their shoes.[45] Some may have even felt that even though he was alive, he was a good Indian.

Although Geronimo "tried his best to be happy and contented," he told Howard that many of his tribe were sick from the bad air and bad water.[46] The interpreter informed Geronimo that there would be no peace in Arizona if the Indians went back to the Chiricahua Mountains. The Great Father in Washington did not have sufficient power to ensure that the Mexicans and white people would treat them fairly. According to Howard, since Geronimo had become a Christian, he was "trying to understand our civilization and, at last, after many years, Geronimo, the last Apache chief, was happy and joyful, for he had learned to try and be good to everybody and to love his white brothers."[47] Geronimo did not express this in *his* story.

---

[42] "SB-17 Office of Racial Equity," accessed October 18, 2021, https://leginfo.legislature.ca.gov/faces/billCompareClient.xhtml?bill_id=202120220SB17&showamends=false,.

[43] Ibid.

[44] O. O. Howard, *Famous Indians I Have Known*, (New York: The Century Co., 1916; accessed on October 18, 2020, at Heritage History https://www.heritage-history.com/index.php?c=read&author=howard&book=chiefs&story=geronimo).

[45] Ibid.

[46] Ibid.

[47] Howard, *Famous Indians I Have Known*.

Chief Joseph, Nez Pierce
National Archives (106-IN-205)

Geronimo learned that even his hero, Major General Howard, had followed military orders to pursue and displace Native Americans. Howard had accepted the surrender of Chief Joseph of the Nez Perce[48] tribe and forced their displacement from some 17 million acres in what is now Montana, Idaho, Washington, and Oregon to a 750,000 acre reservation in Idaho. This was one more trail of tears.

---

[48] The Nez Perce call themselves Nimiipuu, which means "The People." The name "Nez Perce" ("pierced nose") came from French Canadian fur traders. The identification was erroneous as nose piercing was never practiced by the tribe. Additional information can be found at "Nez Perce Tribe," Columbia River Inter-Tribal Fish Commission, https://critfc.org/member-tribes-overview/nez-perce-tribe/#:~:text=The%20Nez%20Perce%20tribe%20was,made%20up%20the%20tribe's%20homeland.

Chapter 7:

Native Americans Learn the Tricks of the Trade

Geronimo with Bow and Arrow
Wikimedia Commons, acessed October 19, 2021

It did not take Geronimo long to acquire a knack for salesmanship. After their reluctant return to Oklahoma, the Apache lived in villages out on the range where they were expected to farm and raise livestock. They did well with cattle and horses and had been led to understand that the money they earned would be given to them. It was never clear to Geronimo what happened to the money that was diverted to an "Apache Fund." It was not until 1980 that the U.S. Congress approved a plan to distribute six million dollars to the Chiricahua Apache Tribes based on 1913 census data.[49] According to the plan, 69% of the award went to the Mescalero Apache Tribe of New Mexico and the remaining 31% to the Fort Sill Apache Indian Tribe of Oklahoma.

---

[49] U.S. Department of the Interior, Indian Affairs, "Apache Judgement Plan is Published," February 6, 1980, https://www.bia.gov/as-ia/opa/online-press-release/apache-judgment-plan-published. Congress approved the plan in 1980, but made the plan effective as of December 20, 1979.

Geronimo taught himself to make canes from different sorts of wood that could be painted and sold. During the last few years of his life, the old warrior lived at various places on the reservation and would make bows, arrows, and other items to sell.

In 1901, Geronimo attended the Pan American Exposition in Buffalo, New York. He was often asked to exhibit his skill with the bow and accepted the offer as long as a nickel was the target and was to be his should he hit it. His marksmanship was good and there were few failures.

Geronimo and Apaches at the St. Louis Fair
Library of Congress (LOT 12980; Control Number 99471922)

In 1904, the Louisiana Purchase Exposition, more widely known as the St. Louis World's Fair, was also a success for the entrepreneurial Geronimo. *The Oklahoman* reported that Geronimo was willing to be part of the big show, but he must have "something like five thousand a night, a shower of bouquets after each act, carriage to and from the theater, and an oyster supper with the manager after the performance."[50] Geronimo

---

[50] "The Story of Geronimo and Oklahoma," Genealogy Trails, accessed May 31, 2022 and based on an article in *The Oklahoman*, April 17, 1904, p. 20, http://genealogytrails.com/oka/Geronimo.html

participated in the fair in 1904, and he stayed in St. Louis for six months. He reported selling his photograph for twenty-five cents (of which he was allowed to keep ten cents) and writing his name for ten, fifteen, or twenty-five cents, keeping all of the money, and making "as much as two dollars a day."[51]

Geronimo realized that American audiences were eager to part with their money in order to be entertained by an old Indian. He was said to have nearly $10,000 in his bank account at the time of his death.[52]

Geronimo in Theodore Roosevelt's Inaugural Parade
National Archives. Library of Congress, Control Number 2010648697

In 1905, Geronimo was one of six Indians who rode in Theodore Roosevelt's inaugural parade. Five of them are shown, left to right, in a famous photo of Roosevelt's Inaugural Parade: Buckskin Charlie (Ute), American Horse (Oglala Sioux), Quanah Parker (Comanche), Geronimo (Chiricahua Apache), and Hollow Horn Bear (Brule Sioux). The sixth participant has been identified as Little Plume (Blackfeet).[53]

---

[51] Barrett, *Geronimo's Story of His Life*, 197.

[52] Bob Boze Bell, "The Glorious and Tragic Last Days of Geronimo", *True West*, November 2019, https://truewestmagazine.com/article/the-glorious-tragic-last-days-of-geronimo/

[53] Jesse Rhodes, "Indians on the Inaugural March," January 14, 2009, https://www.smithsonianmag.com/history/indians-on-the-inaugural-march-46032118/.

Sitting Bull (Tatonka-I-Yatanka)
National Archives (111-SC-85728)

Sitting Bull was another Native American who took advantage of the white man's thirst to learn more of Indian heroes. Like Geronimo and Cochise, his name had become a household word and large audiences would pay to see him and watch him perform. Sitting Bull was a big attraction in the *Wild West* show of Buffalo Bill Cody.

Some American Indians feared that they had angered their gods and that the gods had punished them by putting them on reservations. They had abandoned a spiritual dance referred to as the Ghost Dance, an Indian religious ceremony that was believed to be followed by a return of the dead and a restoration of Native America. Worried that participation by Sitting Bull would incite unrest, Indian police sent officers to rouse Sitting Bull from his bed and arrest him at his home on the Standing Rock reservation in South Dakota. He was said to have resisted arrest and was killed.[54]

Before his death, Sitting Bull inquired,

> What treaty have the Sioux made with the white man that we have broken? Not one. What treaty have the white man ever made with us that they have kept? Not one. When I was a boy the Sioux owned the world; the sun rose and set on their land; they sent ten thousand men to battle. Where are the warriors today? Who slew them? Where are our lands? Who owns them? What law have I broken? Is it wrong for me to love my own? Is it wicked for me because my skin is red? Because I am a Sioux; because I was born where my father lived; because I would die for my people and my country?[55]

Two weeks after Sitting Bull's death, the US Army was sent to stop the Ghost Dance movement and massacred a tribe of Sioux at Wounded Knee, on the Pine Ridge Indian Reservation in South Dakota.[56] This was another example of the sentiment of many that the only a good Indian was a dead Indian. It took one hundred years for both houses of Congress to pass a resolution expressing "deep regret" for the incident. The expression has done little to provide support for honoring promises and treaties made with the Native American population.

---

[54] History.com Editors, "Sitting Bull, updated October 12, 2019, https://www.history.com/topics/native-american-history/sitting-bull

[55] "Sitting Bull Quotes," Quotes.net, accessed October 18, 2021, https://www.quotes.net/quote/17545.

[56] History.com Editors, "Wounded Knee," updated May 29, 2019, https://www.history.com/topics/native-american-history/wounded-knee.

Chapter 8:

THE MISSIONARIES

LeRoy Koopman, a writer and editor for the Reformed Church in America, devoted six years of his life to documenting the attempts by Reformed Church missionaries to lead Native American Indians to a "new Road, the Jesus Road…that would lead them to a better life on earth and a life in heaven when they died."[57] His book, *Taking the Jesus Road,* attempts to present an objective account of the trials and tribulations of those missionaries who dedicated themselves to bring the white man's religion to the Indians. Koopman shares his disappointment in having to record some very unpleasant details as he does his best to relate the facts as he understands them. He goes back more than four centuries and provides historical background material that makes the events of the Oklahoma mission more understandable.

Koopman takes us back to 1624, when the Dutch West Indies Company announced that settlers should "seek to draw the Indians and other blind people to the Knowledge of God and His Word."[58] Henry Hudson had sailed up the river, which now bears his name, in 1609 and the Dutch established colonies (patroons). The colonies were permitted to purchase land and then invite colonists from the Netherlands to settle and work as tenants. One suspects that the question of whose land was being sold did not weigh heavily on the consciences of the buyers or the settlers. Peter Minuit, director of the Dutch North American Colony of New Netherlands, purchased Manhattan Island for a box of trade goods for the legendary $24; however, the concept of ceding land for posterity was not part of the Indian culture. Indians never intended to "sell" and lose *their* land forever.

---

[57] LeRoy Koopman, *Taking the Jesus Road: The Ministry of the Reformed Church in America Among Native Americans* (Michigan: William. B. Eerdmans Publishing Co., 2005), ix.
[58] Koopman, *Taking the Jesus Road: The Ministry of the Reformed Church in America Among Native Americans,* 62.

The area around what is now Albany and Schenectady, New York, was a center of activity. In the late seventeenth century, the Albany church proudly recorded the baptism of 125 Indians. The original Dutch interest in Indian evangelism soon faded as the settlers continued to displace the Indians from their land. Almost 300 years later, this area would be the home of my grandparents, Howard and Abbie Furbeck.

Mission efforts by the Reformed Church in America among American Indians ceased at the time of the American Revolution and would not resume for one hundred and fifty years. It took the women of the Dutch Reformed Church to initiate interest and support for adding domestic missions to the existing foreign mission program. In 1895, Dr. Frank Hall Wright, the son of a Choctaw man and a member of the Choctaw tribe, was sent into the field to evangelize the Indians. This was a remarkable event in that Wright was seriously ill and appeared to be a dying man, suffering from the early stages of tuberculosis.[59] Jason Betzinez, in his book, *I Fought With Geronimo*, remembers Wright as a "trained singer who had studied for grand opera and been offered a place with an opera company in New York."[60]

Policies and practices made missionary work difficult, dangerous, and often discouraging. Wright, who was felt to be at death's door, left his wife and children in Texas and set off to bring the Gospel to the Indians, including Geronimo's band of Chiricahua Apache, who were held as prisoners of war at the Fort Sill military installation.[61] Military authorities initially denied the missionary entrance to the prisoner of war camp, so Wright instead began his work in Colony, Oklahoma, where he eventually installed Reverend Walter C. Roe and his wife. Ultimately Dr. Wright prevailed and, in 1899, the mission among the Apache prisoners at Fort Sill was opened at Mr. Wright's earnest petition, "because no religious work was done for those poor prisoners of war."[62] Wright remained active until his death in 1922.

The Reformed Church realized that this was a critical time for the Indians. Mrs. Roe reported to the Church,

> There is certainly a future for this country, if only the force of civilization does not wipe our poor people off the face of the earth before they have time to learn the white man's ways and

---

[59] Betzinez, *I Fought With Gernomio*, 171.
[60] Betzinez, *I Fought With Geronimo*, 164.
[61] Richard H. Harper, *Chronicles of Oklahoma*, Volume 18, No. 4 December, 1940, "The Missionary Work of the Reformed (Dutch) Church of America, In Oklahoma", Part II Commanches and Apaches, p. 328.
[62] *Twentieth Annual Report of the Women's Executive Committee of the Board of Domestic Missions of the Reformed Church in America for the Year Ending April Thirtieth, 1903* (New York; Board of Publication for the Reformed Church in America), 30

religion. May God give us grace, patience and strength to proclaim His message to them so that they must hear. I feel that their doom or salvation now rests upon their acceptance of Christ. If they reject Him they are lost, not only individually, but as a race. If they accept Him and His gentle Spirit it will be so easy to learn better ways of living, for they surely are law-abiding, except under cruel and unendurable injustice.[63]

The annual report to the Women's Executive Committee of the Board of Domestic Missions for the year ending in April 1899 indicated that thirty-five Indians and two whites had been admitted by profession of faith.[64] That was the good news. Minutes of the church board disclosed that even within that relatively small group, there were those guilty of drunkenness, gambling, immorality, absence from church, and marrying according to the Indian custom[65]. The Jesus Road was not without potholes for the Indians.

We descendants of Howard R. Furbeck (Papa) can recall overhearing recollections of our parents and Gramma Abbie Furbeck of events that had occurred on the mission field in 1900 and 1901, and of the times that Papa spent with Geronimo the Indian. Until his untimely death in 1917, Papa would, on occasion, share pictures in the family albums and tales of what life was like as a missionary. It took an extensive search to find information that would document the "rest of the story," and a written account of the role Grandfather Furbeck played as a missionary with the goal of convincing Geronimo to "take the Jesus Road."

In June 1941, Richard H. Harper wrote an article entitled "The Missionary Work of the Reformed (Dutch) Church in America, in Oklahoma. Part III, Work Among White People," in *The Chronicles of Oklahoma*. This was the link that provided the Furbeck family with a description of what their grandfather had accomplished on the mission field and his relationship with Geronimo. Harper wrote:

> The Reformed Church in America had entered this Indian country in 1895, to work with the red men, and did not plan to establish work among white people. However, as the years went by requests were made of this denomination to place ministers in localities inhabited by whites.

---

[63] *Sixteenth Annual Report of the Women's Executive Committee of the Board of Domestic Missions of the Reformed Church in America for the Year Ending April Thirtieth, 1899* (New York: Press of E. Scott Co.), 30
[64] *Sixteenth Annual Report of the Women's Executive Committee of the Board of Domestic Missions of the Reformed Church in America for the Year Ending April Thirtieth, 1899*, 31
[65] Koopman, *Taking the Jesus Road: The Ministry of the Reformed Church Among Native Americans*, 83.

Responding to this call from the west, in June, 1900, four young men who were theological students in the Reformed Church Seminary in New Brunswick, New Jersey, were sent to Oklahoma by the Board of Domestic Missions of the Reformed Church in America, whose headquarters were, and now are, in New York City. The young men sent to this new mission field in the west were John Meengs, P. P. Cheff, T. Mulder, and Howard Furbeck.[66]

Howard Furbeck at the Reformed Church Seminary
Furbeck family photograph

Harper then goes on to describe the multiple challenges that confronted these young men who left their comfortable surroundings in New Jersey wearing suits and ties and heading for what was then the western

---

[66] Richard Harper, *Chronicles of Oklahoma*, Volume 19, No. 2, Missionary Work of the Reformed (Dutch) Church in America, In Oklahoma, Part III, Work Among White People, p. 170, accessed October 20, 2021 at https://gateway.okhistory.org. Reformed Church records report the full names of Howard Furbeck's fellow missionaries as John Gerardus Meengs, Peter Paul Chef d'Hotel, and Ties Mulder.

frontier, armed with a desire to save souls. Harper reports that "the big four" arrived by train in Mountain View on June 1, 1900, before traveling to Colony to work under the direction of Dr. Walter C. Roe.[67]

The "Big Four"
Furbeck family photograph

This work represented "a new departure" in Western work and was described in a 1900 Board of Domestic Missions Report.

> Four missionaries are to be sent to Oklahoma; not to work among the Indians, but among the people in the new little towns which have sprung up along the line of railroad gradually approaching Colony; and which are, along certain lines, a menace to the work our dear missionaries are doing for the Indians. Last year Mr. Roe asked that at least one student be sent to the one town there. Now there are three of these typical frontier towns, which grow up "in a night." Perhaps before the summer is over there may be another added to the three; so, in order to be "first on the ground," if that should be, we have decided to send four students.

---

[67] Richard Harper, in "Work Among the White People," reports that the team was under the supervision of Walter E. Roe. This is believed to be a typographical error. In his book, *I Fought With Geronimo*, Jason Betzinez credits Dr. Walter C. Roe and Dr. Frank H. Wright as establishing the mission of the Dutch Reformed Church and leading the work at Colony.

It is altogether too soon to speak of their work. The conditions differ from our regular student work, and must be met differently. Until the students are at their posts (which will be early in June), we can report nothing. But we beg you to follow them with your prayers as they go to their places amid strange surroundings, where the work will be one requiring infinite tact and wisdom, for which they must look constantly to their great Leader. These students are all good musicians. Their singing (we made it a stipulation that all should sing) and playing will be a most important factor; for they may sing the Gospel to some who would scorn the spoken word.[68]

Harper provides a similar account, stating that the four student missionaries were sent to work "not among the Indians or Hollanders, but among the cowboys and ranchmen living along the line of the railroad which gradually approaches Colony.[69]"

Howard Rutsen Furbeck, Missionary
Furbeck family photograph

---

[68] *Seventeenth Annual Report of the Women's Executive Committee of the Board of the Domestic Missions of the Reformed Church in America for the Year Ending April 20th, 1900* (New Jersey: The Cranford Citizen), 17-18.
[69] *Acts and Proceedings of the General Synod of the Reformed Church in America, Vol. XIX, Embracing the Period from June, 1898, to June, 1901, Inclusive* (New York: New York Board of Publication of the Reformed Church in America, 19010, 759

Once out West, derby hats disappeared and were replaced with wide-brimmed sombreros. Included among their baggage were Mulder's violin and Furbeck's guitar. It took little time to equip them for their itinerant work with a Studebaker wagon covered with canvas and resembling a prairie schooner, two Indian ponies to pull the wagon, cots to sleep on, pots to cook in, and a plate, knife, and fork.

Prairie Schooner
Furbeck family photograph

Their job description was not complicated. They were to take advantage of every opportunity to convince their audience to become Christians. Mulder used his violin, Furbeck his guitar, and Meengs was the principal evangelist. They met with success as some in the crowds accepted their invitation. Rarely did they spend more than ten days in one location.

H.R. Furbeck with Guitar
Furbeck family photo

Although the quartet was sent to reach out to "the cowboys and ranchmen," the Women's Executive Committee of the Board of the Domestic Missions of the Reformed Church noted that

> Two camp meetings were held last Summer, one in July for the Cheyennes and Arapahoes, the other in August for the Apaches. At both meetings great assistance was rendered by the Oklahoma Student Quartette, the young men kindly arranging their other work so that they might be present on these occasions. There were large audiences at both meetings, and several confessed their faith in Christ, while the Christian Indians were encouraged to renewed efforts, for they frequently meet with disfavor and coldness from their own people whose hearts are still turned from the Gospel.[70]

A more vivid description was published in *The Christian Intelligencer* in a report from Colony that describes a camp meeting that began on Thursday evening, June 28, and closed Sabbath evening, July 1.

> The annual camp meeting has just concluded, and of it I wish to write. It was held on a level, wooded stretch of pasture circled by Cobb Creek. Shade was plentiful, and springs of fresh water were near. Between six and seven hundred Indians gathered to the feast. Rations of beef, flour, coffee, sugar and lard were issued, the money for this being largely contributed by the Endeavor Society of the Second Collegiate Church of Harlem. The Indians were mostly Cheyennes and Arapahoes, with a band of visiting Kiowas.

> Imagine a central arbor of staunch uprights, notched at the top and covered with poles and boughs. Clustering around this are tepees, tents and touchups. Canvas-covered wagons, hacks and buggies stand everywhere about. Horses, ponies and mules are tethered here and there or roam about at will, feeding on the abundant mesquite and sedge grasses. Groups of men and women stand or sit near the tepees and tents. Cooking fires are alight. Children play about. Dogs snarl and bark. All is life, stir, and animation. Bright colors show. Blankets and shawls, deerskin and calico suits, ornaments and trinkets present a harmonious mingling of reds, blues, yellows, greens in squares, plaids, stripes, flowers and tracery.

---

[70] *Eighteenth Annual Report of the Women's Executive Committee of the Board of the Domestic Missions of the Reformed Church in America for the Year Ending April Thirteenth, 1901* (New York: The Board of Publication of the Reformed Church in America), 19-20.

A large hand bell is rung under the arbor—service time has come. Mrs. Roe plays on the organ. One of the New Brunswick students plays his violin. We all join in the singing. A group of school girls, most of them members of our church, comes quietly in. They are very neat and pretty and very picturesque in their bright blankets and shawls. With an Indian woman's inimitable grace they seat themselves on a large blanket laid on the grass before the organ. Hartley, the Arapahoe interpreter, is in his Place to the left. Little Chief, the Cheyenne, stands straight near a post to the right to interpret the sermons to his people.[71]

The report goes on to describe the service, with prayers made in English, Cheyenne, and Arapahoe. After prayers arrives "the quartette of seniors from New Brunswick Seminary, Messrs. Furbeck, Meengs, Mulder, and Cheff. Mr. Roe or Mr. Wright preaches and others of us add testimonies. An invitation is given to inquirers to come forward. Wautan, the Arapahoe elder, speaks earnestly to his people. Little Chief speaks to the Cheyennes. A little group of penitents forms before the organ, and then we talk and pray with the anxious individuals."[72]

Three services were held each day at the camp meeting. It was a success. "On Sabbath morning the consistory met, and eight were added by baptism to the church."[73]

The Women's Executive Committee of the Board of the Domestic Missions noted the quartet's "excellent service" in their annual report.

> The four students sent to Oklahoma last summer did such excellent service that they are to be returned to that field; though now they will go as ordained missionaries, and able to do a far greater work. Where opportunity offers they are to organize churches in some of the frontier towns springing up along the line of railway, which is so slowly but surely nearing Colony, one of our Indian mission stations in Oklohoma [*sic*]; and which in some ways are proving both a menace and a temptation to our Christian Indians. In these towns there are neither churches nor settled pastors; the way is clear; the door open, and our Church may enter if she will. God grant that those beloved young missionaries may plant our banner there! They wish very much to establish "reading rooms" in all the towns—fifteen at least—to be preaching (in a way) after their preaching is over.[74]

---

[71] Rev. W.M. Justin Marsha, D. D., "God Speaking to Simple Hearts," *The Christian Intelligencer*, July 18, 1900, 460.

[72] Ibid.

[73] Ibid.

[74] *Eighteenth Annual Report of the Women's Executive Committee of the Board of the Domestic Missions of the Reformed Church in America for the Year Ending April Thirteenth, 1901*, 14.

The report then went on to appeal for reading material to be sent to keep towns supplied with the best magazines and up-to-date papers the whole year round.

After three months on the mission front, the four missionaries returned to New Brunswick, put on their suits and ties, and completed their theological courses at New Brunswick Theological Seminary. Howard Furbeck also began courting Abbie Rollins.

1901 Graduating Class, New Brunswick Theological Seminary
Furbeck family photograph. Howard Furbeck is seated in the second row, second from left.

In 1901, Kiowa, Comanche, Wichita, and Caddo nations were involuntarily transplanted from their homelands and assigned to reservation life in Fort Sill, Oklahoma. According to Harper's account, when the "big four" returned to Oklahoma for Christian service in the summer of 1901, they made their "headquarters" at the Fort Sill Apache Indian Mission of the Reformed Church, located on the Fort Sill military reservation, where Apache, including Geronimo, were being held as prisoners of war by the United States Government. They were warmly welcomed by the commanding officer of the post and spent their first week working with the soldiers and meeting with other missionaries.

Howard Furbeck on the Porch
Furbeck family photograph·

After their first week, they went south. Travel was sometimes difficult because of lack of water, even for the horses. As described in Harper's account, "The poor animals would pull the wagon for many miles, uphill and down, in the terrific heat, where they were almost parched for water. Among the places visited were Martha, Dott, Warren, Mangum, Duncan, Marlow, and the place where Lawton suddenly came into being. So far only the name 'Lawton' existed, except for a shanty labeled 'Land Office.' "[75]

---

[75] Harper, "Work Among the White People," 171

"Towns" On the Missionary Trail
Furbeck family photographs

Harper reports that outside the town site, "thousands" were waiting, and one of the young missionaries described the crowd as consisting of "Jews, gentiles, black, white, Indian, Mexican, gamblers, prostitutes, saloon keepers, good people, bad people, cutthroats and soldiers."[76]

Harper further reports that men in uniform were needed to preserve order and

> Every night for more than a week they preached and sang the Gospel story. Each evening Rev. Frank Hall Wright, the Indian evangelist of the Reformed Church, came from the Apache Mission a few miles away. The Gospel wagon would drive up close to a crowd. Immediately the violin and guitar could be heard, followed by the quartet as they sang "Where is My Wandering Boy Tonight," or "Tell Mother I'll Be There," or some other favorite. A short sermon followed by Dr. Wright, a forceful message going deep into the hearts of the listeners. After the sermon came a song of invitation by the quartet, an exhortation and a prayer; and the meeting ended.[77]

Gospel Services; All Welcome
Furbeck family photograph

---

[76] Ibid.

[77] Ibid.

Prairie Pulpit
Furbeck family photograph

A successful feature of the mission program was the camp meeting. Indian dances had always been popular in bringing together families that were widely scattered in camps; the camp meeting was intended to be a Christian version of those gatherings. The first camp meeting was held in 1897, but in 1901 a "great feast" was added and the camp meeting became an integral part of the mission.[78]

In her book, *In Camp and Tepee,* Elizabeth M. Page depicts a day early in the summer of 1901 when the full-timers were accompanied by "four of these young men," one of whom was my grandfather. She describes how the men spent an hour "snugging down" their camp, unhitching the horses, unloading the wagons, and tossing tents, cots, rolls of bedding while handling "with tender care" the chuck-box and sheet-iron cooking stove.[79]

---

[78] Koopman, *Taking the Jesus Road: The Ministry of the Reformed Church in America Among Native Americans*, 85.
[79] Elizabeth M. Page, *In Camp and Tepee, An Indian Mission Story* (New York: The Board of Publication and Bible-School Work of the Reformed Church in America, 1915), 98.

Dining at Camp
Furbeck family photograph

Howard Furbeck Surveys the Tents
Furbeck family photograph

While on the mission field with his guitar, Howard shared his lifetime goals with Abbie Rollins, the love of his life. He sensed an obligation to let her know that, for the foreseeable future Abbie and their future children could be sharing him with the mission field. She must understand him, and his calling, and be willing to continue to understand.

Poetry and music were important components of his courtship. While in Oklahoma, Howard Furbeck composed a poem for Abbie, which he set to music. He wrote:

Abbie Rollins
Furbeck family photograph

A homeless wanderer, forever seeking I stray

Fate divine leads the way

Seeking, seeking but seeking in vain

For one, the one, her love to claim

That fond ideal of the heart

To call my own 'til death shall part

Full oft have I gazed at the throng of earth

Drifting away on the stream of mirth

Methinks I at last have found the one

The one I am to call my own

Visions of the future come to my mind

At last the seeker has sought to find

Through surviving correspondence, we learn that the quartet made an impact on many souls. On July 29, 1901, Abbie Rollins mentioned the important work the quartet was doing in the field. "My dear Mr. Furbeck," she wrote, "We are so pleased to hear of the success with which you are meeting in your work, thirty souls born into the Kingdom of God, and so much seed dropped to bear fruit in the days to come, of which you may never know here, but which Christ himself will reveal to you when all work here is finished." Could one of those souls have been Geronimo's?

Missionaries in the field
Furbeck family photograph

There is no shortage of reports of Geronimo's conversion to Christianity.[80] Geronimo confirmed his Christianity in his story to Asa Daklugie, a nephew of Geronimo's, who translated Geronimo's story for S. M. Barrett. Barrett's account includes this statement from Geronimo:

> "Since my life as a prisoner has begun I have heard the teachings of the white man's religion, and in many respects believe it to be better than the religion of my fathers. However, I have always prayed, and I believe that the Almighty has always protected me. Believing that in a wise way it is good to go to church, and that associating with Christians would improve my

---

[80] In addition to the account published here, *The Oklahoman* reported on page six of the July 16, 1903 edition that Geronimo "became a Methodist" the previous Sunday. The paper reported that the service took place "in the tabernacle of Medicine, with the Comanches sitting upon the ground on the one side and the Apaches on the other, each tribe with its interpreter standing in the foreground repeating the message of the pale face." The article also states that "At 2 o'clock on the same day, in the midst of a multitude of people, the minister sprinkled the clear water over the old chief's head and repeated; "in the name of the father and of the Son and of the Holy Ghost," and Geronimo became a Methodist". This author and others disagree with this account.

character, I have adopted the Christian religion. I believe that the church has helped me much during the short time I have been a member. I am not ashamed to be a Christian, and am glad to know that the President of the United States is a Christian for without the help of the Almighty I do not think he could rightly judge in ruling so many people I have advised all of my people who are not Christians, to study that religion, because it seems to me the best religion in enabling one to live right."[81]

Reports of Geronimo's interest in Christianity appear as early as November 12, 1889, when *The New York Times* reported that at the seventh annual meeting of the New York Indian Association, a statement was made that Geronimo had embraced Christianity and was engaged in Sunday school work.[82] LeRoy Koopman, who chronicled the ministry of the Reformed Church in America among Native Americans, reports that Geronimo was baptized in 1903 after hearing the Reverend J. Tallmadge Bergen, a professor at Hope College, preach in the field in July of that year.[83]

In her book, *In Camp and Tepee*, Elizabeth Page describes where Geronimo first professed his faith to Dr. Wright and Dr. Bergen as a field with a gospel tent spread "under the great shadowy trees of the oak Grove on the bend of Medicine Creek."[84] In this account, the baptism did not take place until after Dr. Roe had a chance to question Geronimo regarding his faith. On completing his questioning, Roe stated that "no consistory in our church could refuse to admit a man to membership after such a confession."[85] Page reports that "a week later Geronimo was baptized with six others."[86] The baptism was also written up in the July 24, 1903 edition of the *Ottawa County Times* on page one under the headline "Indian Chief Baptized." In this account, the baptism was described as taking place on July 12, with Rev. Wright performing the ceremony at Fort Sill after Dr. Bergan delivered a sermon. The article goes on to say that "at that time 14 other Indians were also baptized."[87]

[81] Barrett, *Geronimo's Story of His Life*, p. 207. Barrett reports that Geronimo was baptized into the Dutch Reformed Church in the summer of 1903 in footnote 57.
[82] "They Converted Geronimo; Statement Made by the New York Indian Association," *The New York Times*, November 12, 1889, 8.
[83] Koopman, *Taking the Jesus Road*, 117.
[84] Page, *In Camp and Tepee: An Indian Mission Story*, 144.
[85] Ibid, 146.
[86] Ibid.
[87] "Indian Chief Baptized, Ottawa County Times, July 24, 1903, 1.

Howard Rutsen Furbeck's children learned that their father was the person who baptized Geronimo in a ceremony captured on film.

Howard Rutsen Furbeck Baptizing Geronimo
Furbeck family photograph

In addition to the Furbeck family photograph, the 1902 *Report of Committee on Indian Work* began its annual report with a description of the 1901 camp meeting, where "many souls" were awakened, and which Rev. Furbeck attended.

> Let us begin the story, then, with the camp meeting of last July, held near the Apache Mission at Fort Sill. Mr. and Mrs. Roe drove down from Colony with a number of Cheyennes and Arapahoes. Mr. Wright, as well as the Oklahoma Quartette joined the party, and the best meeting ever held was soon in progress. The visible results were apparent in the awakening of many souls to a knowledge of Gospel truths, but other lives as well were quickened, and hearts encouraged by loving fellowship and sympathy.[88]

This summer was eventful for Rev. Furbeck in other ways as well. While on July 29, 1901, Abbie Rollins wrote to "My dear Mr. Furbeck," on November 14, 1901 Abbie wrote to "Dear Howard" and mentions wedding preparations. The couple was married in a ceremony covered by *The New York Times*, which reported that the

---

[88] *Nineteenth Annual Report of the Women's Executive Committee of the Board of the Domestic Missions of the Reformed Church in America for the Year Ending April Thirtieth, 1902* (New York: The Board of Publication of the Reformed Church in America), 29.

celebration was enough to stop two express trains.[89] *The Christian Intelligencer* gave a more conventional account of the wedding, stating that it took place on Wednesday, November 27, 1901, at the First Presbyterian Church of New Brunswick, New Jersey[90].

During the early years of their marriage, there were frequent moves. Howard served the Amsterdam (1901-1903) and Rensselaer (1903-1907) Reformed churches in upstate New York, and the Addisville (1908-1912) Reformed Church in Richboro, Pennsylvania, before finally responding to a call from Annandale, New Jersey, where he lived with Abbie and his children. He also continued to write and publish music[91].

WEDDING FIRE STOPS TRAINS.

Red Lights Burned to Speed the Departing Couple Alarms Engineers of Expresses.

Special to The New York Times.

NEW BRUNSWICK, Nov. 30.—Miss Abbie Rollins was married yesterday to the Rev. Howard Furbeck and a crowd accompanied them to the railroad station. A dozen boxes of red fire candles were set blazing just as two express trains were due.

The first to arrive was the east-bound express. When the engineer saw the glare of red he thought that something terrible had happened and that the signal was meant for him. He put on the brakes and brought the train up with a sharp jerk.

Hardly had that train got around the curve before the west-bound express came through, and the performance was repeated. Then the station hands charged upon the red-fire burners and suppressed them and the candles.

Abbie and Howard at Home
Furbeck family photograph

[89] "Wedding Fire Stops Trains. Red Lights Burned to Speed the Departing Couple Alarms Engineers of Expresses," special in the *New York Times*, December 1, 1901, 1.

[90] "Marriages," *New The Christian Intelligencer*, December 11, 1901, 819.

[91] Howard Furbeck is known to have contributed to three pieces of published music: *Memories* (words by H. R. Furbeck, music by Eugene Kaeffer, 1905), *Springtime After Winter; Flowers After Snow,* published by The Rollins music company, 1912; and *Hail to the Flag; Song to the Flag of our Union,* words and music by H.R Furbeck, arranged by Norman Landis (1916).

Harper reports that by the summer of 1901, the Board of Domestic Missions had decided to begin permanent work in Oklahoma, with two of the men remaining (Cheff and Mulder[92]) for the work, while two, having already accepted calls to Eastern churches (Furbeck and Meengs), returned home. Oral history from the Furbeck family relates that Howard Furbeck may have continued his work in the field, and brought gifts for the family from his mission trips.

Handiwork from the Mission Field
Photo by Peter MacIntosh, used with permission

On October 16, 1917, Howard Furbeck was killed while riding his bicycle after being struck by an automobile. The widow and their five children (Rollins, fourteen; Marion, twelve; Lucille, seven; Dorothy, five; and Anita, three) mourned his death but, despite a difficult financial situation, always spoke reverently of Papa.

---

[92] According to the *New York Times* (November 20, 1901), Rev. Ties Mulder won a tract of land fronting on the river, near Liberty, Oklahoma, after registering for a government land lottery. His fiancée, Miss Elizabeth Lauber of New Brunswick, joined him in Oklahoma, where they were married on Thanksgiving Day at Liberty, where Mulder had already established a small church.

Rollins, Marion, Lucille, and Dorothy Furbeck
Furbeck family photograph

Geronimo's cousin, Jason Betzinez, also became a Christian. The families of Geronimo and Betzinez were held as prisoners of war on the Fort Sill reservation. Both families escaped; however Betzinez recognized the futility of the situation and returned to the reservation. Betzinez perfected his English and became a blacksmith as well as a sergeant in the US Army Indian Scouts. He eventually built his own home off the reservation and had a successful blacksmith business.

The school and orphanage at Fort Sill were served by both missionary wives and many unmarried women, who found this an opportunity to evangelize the Indians, and also to find husbands who shared their faith. Betzinez was a charter member of the Apache Christian Endeavor Society, was elected treasurer in 1900, and made recording secretary in 1906. In 1907, this Indian, who had fought with Geronimo, met Anna Heersma, a Dutch Reformed Missionary, and fell in love. Too shy to reveal his feelings, it was twelve years before he proposed. Their marriage lasted forty-one years.

Geronimo and Betzinez are buried next to each other in the Beef Creek Apache Cemetery in Lawton, Oklahoma. The obituary of Geronimo, as reported on February 17 and printed in the February 18, 1909 *New York Times,* mentions that "He will be buried in the Indian cemetery tomorrow by the missionaries, the old chief having professed religion three years ago."[93]

---

[93] "Old Apache Chief Geronimo is Dead," On This Day, February 19, 1909. Special to the New York Times, https://archive.nytimes.com/www.nytimes.com/learning/general/onthisday/bday/0616.html.

Chapter 9:

THE CONTROVERSY CONTINUES

In 1905, S. M. Barrett asked the officer in charge at Fort Sill, Lieutenant Purington, for permission to publish Geronimo's autobiography. Permission was promptly denied. It was made clear that Geronimo and his warriors deserved to be hanged rather than receive so much attention from civilians. Barrett then wrote to President Theodore Roosevelt to obtain permission for the old Indian to tell his side of the story.

President Theodore Roosevelt
National Archives (559330)

Barrett submitted his manuscript to the president in 1906. Roosevelt wrote, "This is a very interesting volume which you have in manuscript but I would advise that you disclaim responsibility in all cases where the reputation of an individual is assailed."[94] Barrett adjusted his manuscript, and submitted it to the War Department on June 2, 1906. Six weeks after submission, Thomas C. Barry, Brigadier General, Assistant to the Chief of Staff, sent a note to the president advising that "the document, either in whole or in part, should

---
[94] Barrett, *Geronimo's Story of His Life*, p. xxiii.

not receive the approval of the War Department."[95] With the president's support, permission was ultimately granted, and Barrett's final product made the objections of the War Department known.

It is not possible to record all of the incidents that affect the sensibilities of tribal nations. Too few non-Native Americans are aware of the concept of tribal sovereignty. There has been a disconnect about what tribal sovereignty means, but the bottom line is that Native Americans have been engaged in a continuous struggle to get the United States to live up to its treaty obligations. After centuries of war, relocation, removal, and assimilation (attempts at genocide), many tribes no longer have rights to natural resources in their original homelands. Without these rights, how do these people who have become dependent become self-dependent?

For example, the San Carlos Apache have always considered their land to be sacred. Rio Tinto PLC covets a rich vein of copper on land belonging to the San Carlos Apache for the Resolution Copper Project. In December 2014, Congress passed the National Defense Authorization Act, which approved a land transfer to give Rio Tinto access to the copper deposit. Congressional hearings conducted on March 12, 2020, vividly describe the irreparable environmental and cultural impacts of the proposed mining operation on land that, according to testimony, "has been explicitly protected from mining interests since 1955, when President Dwight D. Eisenhower withdrew it from potential development."[96] A statement from the Honorable Ruben Gallego, a representative in Congress from the state of Arizona, described the impact in public testimony:

> This technique will create a massive crater that will directly and permanently damage the Oat (sic) Flat area. The crater is projected to start to appear in Year 6 of active mining and will ultimately be between 800 and 1,100 feet deep and roughly 1.8 miles across. If you want to try to picture that, this mine will create a hole that is twice as deep as the Washington Monument is tall and that will stretch the distance between the U.S. Capitol and the Lincoln Memorial.

> And in this crater of destruction will be the sacred site of the Apache people. In this crater will be the ancient Emery Oak Groves, which have been used by tribal members for millennia. In this crater will be the ancestral burial grounds of the Indigenous peoples of Southern Arizona. As there has never been a complete survey of the area, it is difficult to know exactly how many

---

[95] Barrett, *Geronimo's Story of His Life*, p. xxv.

[96] "The Irreparable Environmental and Cultural Impacts of the proposed Resolution Copper Mining Project," Oversight Hearing before the Committee on Natural Resources, U.S. House of Representatives, One Hundred Sixteenth Congress, Second Session, March 12, 2020, https://www.congress.gov/event/116th-congress/house-event/LC65246/text?s=1&r=1.

cultural resources may be destroyed or swallowed by this crater. But it is not hard to know the hurt and trauma this will inflict on the Native people who hold this place sacred. In addition to the destruction of sacred sites, this mine will have impacts that would last for centuries.

Unchecked groundwater pumping would deplete the area of water resources, contributing to a water shortage crisis that Arizona is already grappling with and depleting sacred springs in that area. The operation will also produce 1.3 billion tons of toxic tailings, which will be pumped through pipelines to a yet-to-be-determined storage facility. [97]

Geronimo would not have OK'd the Resolution Copper Project. The Save Oak Flat Act was introduced by Arizona Congressman Grijalva, and a senate companion by Senators Bernie Sanders and Elizabeth Warren. Sanders commented, "Too many times our Native American brothers and sisters have seen the profits of huge corporations put ahead of their sovereign rights." Geronimo would have agreed.

Skull and Bones
Photo by Peter McIntosh,
used with permission.

On February 19, 2009, *The New York Times* reported that the descendants of Geronimo had sued a Yale secret Society, Skull and Bones, charging that its members had robed Geronimo's grave in 1918 and have his skull on display in a glass case. Prescott Bush, the father of George Bush and grandfather of George W. Bush, was said to have broken into the grave of Geronimo in Oklahoma and made off with artifacts, including the skull, which was then put on display at the clubhouse in New Haven known as The Tomb. The society elects fifteen elite members each year, and in addition to the Bush family includes Senator John Kerry. The suit does not appear to have gone anywhere, is likely more fiction than fact, but put Geronimo in the news. Yale University states the society is independent of the school.

When Al-Qaeda leader Osama bin Laden was killed by Navy Seals in May 2011, reports announced that "Operation Geronimo" had been successful. In response, Harlyn Geronimo, great-grandson of Geronimo, submitted a statement to the official record of the United States Senate Commission on Indian Affairs Oversight Hearing on "Stolen Identities: The Impact of Racist Stereotypes on Indigenous People," which took place on Thursday, May 5, 2011.

---

[97] Ibid.

Whether it was intended only to name the military operation to kill or capture Osama Bin Laden or to give Osama Bin Laden himself the code name Geronimo, either was an outrageous insult and mistake. And it is clear from the military records released that the name Geronimo was used at times by military personnel involved for both the military operation and for Osama Bin Laden himself.

Obviously to equate Geronimo with Osama Bin Laden is an unpardonable slander of Native America and its most famous leader in history.[98]

The plight of Native Americans is unlikely to be resolved by mankind. The question "why me?" or "why us?" can have a different meaning that is dependent upon the effect of an event on the questioner. Throughout North America, one can understand why Job of the Old Testament or, in modern times, the Native American Indians ask God why suffering has been inflicted on them.

In 1972, Kris Kristofferson wrote and recorded a song entitled "Why Me," in which he asked God what he had accomplished in his life to deserve the many gifts he had received. It was a major success. I expect many readers of this book have asked God the same question.

The book of Ecclesiastes 3:14 (NIV) informs its readers that "I know that everything God does will endure forever; nothing can be added to it and nothing taken from it. God does it, so men will revere him." It does not tell us why God continues to allow genocide.

I continue to find inspiration in a sermon I heard in the Hope College Chapel delivered by philosophy professor D. Ivan Dykstra titled "What's So Good About Friday?" He concluded with multiple examples of anguish and agony and informed us that "*By* stripes come healing. *By* hurting we are sainted. *By* dying we can learn to live." [99]

I believe that Howard R. Furbeck, Geronimo, and I would all agree with 1 Corinthians 13:12 (NIV): "Now we see but a poor reflection, then we shall see face to face. Now I know in part: then I shall know fully, even as I am fully known."

---

[98] ICT Staff, "Indian County Responds to Geronimo, bin Laden Connection," *Indian Country Today*, updated September 13, 2018, https://indiancountrytoday.com/archive/indian-country-responds-to-geronimo-bin-laden-connection.

[99] D. Ivan Dysksta, *Who Am I? And Other Sermons from Dimnent Memorial Chapel, Hope College, Holland, Michigan* (Michigan: Hope College, 1983), 20.

A framed copy of a masterpiece, "Crossing the Bar," written by Alfred Tennyson that once hung in my father's study says it better than I could ever hope to.

Twilight and evening bell,

And after that the dark!

And may there be no sadness of farewell,

When I embark;

For tho' from our bourne of Time and Place

The flood may bear me far,

I hope to see my Pilot face to face

When I have crost the bar.

We can say OK to that.

Appendix 1: Correspondence between Howard and Abbie

Theological Seminary
of the
Reformed Church in America.

New Brunswick, N. J., *Oct 31* 1900.

My dear Miss Rollins.

Your note of the 29th was received. I will arrange then to call on Monday evening - November the fifth.

Together with studies and social events I find this week fully occupied, so the evening you suggested will be quite satisfactory.

I have also been trying

Theological Seminary
of the
Reformed Church in America.

New Brunswick, N. J., 1900.

some new experiments in toning and printing. so I will have my collection more complete.

Hoping that no unforeseen circumstances may arise - to alter arrangements -

I am -

Respectfully Yours
H. R. Furbeck

Hertzog Hall –
Dec – 17 – 1900

Dear friend Miss Rollins:–
                    I was never
more surprised than
when last night – I look-
ed at my watch – when
leaving your house and
saw how late was the
hour. I heard the clock
strike in the other
room and thought
it was for ten – it must
have struck eleven instead
But I hope you will
pardon my thoughtlessness

I have been yawning
and gaping in my
recitations to day – but
passed through them
all right.

    I find the examination
schedule is changed
so that Thursday is
not a hard day for
us, so I have changed
my plans in regard
to skating, expecting to
remain in to night
and go Wednesday
night instead. I was
wondering if you would
not like to accompany
me. We could go on the

seven o'clock car and
return by nine.

I have just developed
the 1st flash light and
it came out fine – It
will make an
elegant print.

The mail just came
in and with it a letter
from Rochelle Park –
Land – an invitation to
preach there the 6th
of January.

I have that tin type
in a nice frame and it
shows off lovely

Well I must close as
it. 6 C M

Sincerely – J & R Furbeck

New Brunswick, N.J.
July 29/01.

My dear Mr. Furbeck:-

I received your letter on Saturday, and was indeed glad to hear from you, for it seems a long time since you have written. I am so sorry that you have not received my letters. I have written twice, but addressed them to "Colony", thinking they would reach you all right.

In the first I told you of my Mother's illness, and the next I wrote on the morning of her death. Oh! Mr. Furbeck you don't know how hard it is to tell you of this. She passed away last Sabbath morning, July 21st, about 7 o'clock. And as she closed her eyes and I called, but no answer came, it seemed as though all the world had gone and left me alone. You can understand when I say I always considered my Mother, my all. She was all that made my home, and it is so lonesome without her. I have been staying with my sister ever since. Today is my first day at the office for four weeks. Three weeks I was home with Mother while she was sick, and it is such a comfort now to look back and think about the many pleasant hours we spent together before she got so very sick. But everyone has been so kind and good to us during these sad days; it is indeed a comfort to have so much sympathy bestowed at such a time.

Perhaps sometime, I can tell you more about it, but just now I feel I cannot. I can only say that we know she is safe with Him whom she loved and to whom she longed to go.

We are so pleased to hear of the

success with which you are meeting in your work, thirty souls born into the kingdom of God, and so much seed dropped to bear fruit in the days to come, of which you may never know here, but which Christ himself will reveal to you when all work here is finished. What satisfaction there is in doing and giving our best.

You asked in one of your letters what I thought in regard to your settling in the West, but I have not had time to even think of it. While I was with Mother, I hardly knew day from night, or night from day, and yet I was not tired, I could have kept it up for weeks, if only it would have helped to bring her back to health, but God willed differently.

The tie between Mother and daughter is so close and tender, and grows so much more precious as the years go by, that at times I feel I cannot give her up. But I know that God's claim comes first, and since Mother and Home are so closely connected, perhaps when the dreadful ache is healed just a little (if it ever can be) Heaven will be more homelike because she is there.

There is a great deal in the papers just now in regard to the opening up of the new country in the West. What a wonderful sight it must be.

In my other letters I told you that the College had granted your degree of "B.D." I am sorry that you did not receive these, as it must have seemed very strange not to hear.

Miss Lefferts and Mr. Lane are to be married in about three weeks. They expect to take quite a trip, which will include the Pan American Exposition, and Mr. Lane could get away better at that time than later. They seem, and of course they are, very happy, for I have always believed that they were a truly mated couple.

Well I must close and turn again back to work.

The best part of your last letter was that you would so soon begin to pack up for the East. It will be so good to see you again and hear of your experiences.

With best wishes, I am

Sincerely Yours,

Abbie Rollins.

New Brunswick, N.J.
Nov. 4 - 1901

Dear Howard:-

It does seem strange
to address you in this manner,
but I think it will mean
for us a drawing nearer to each
other. In fact it hardly
seems possible at times, you
and I preparing for our wedding
day, but at times I think I
can catch a glimpse of the

beautiful and divine leading
of our Heavenly Father.

There have been times when
I have felt so incompetent. so
unworthy of taking this high
place at your side, but when
I look up into the face of my
Savior, and remember the prayer
of my life "Lead thy way. into
a broad life of usefullness and
service for thee". he seems to say
"Come this way, Sufficient
for the day shall thy strength be".

And may we be able to say in
the days to come, "Surely the
Lord has led us all the way."

But now in regard to the
important details of the day.

Isn't it nice that you should
have a call from both places,
and I believe. I am truly glad,
that you have accepted Berne.
While of course I know very
little in regard to either place
or people, still my heart seemed
to centre more at Berne, and

my feeling now is that I shall like it.

Your first letter in regard to preparation almost took my breath away. The responsibility of planning and arranging in such a short time quite overwhelmed me, but the nearest date I think for which we could possibly arrange would be the 26th or 27th of November. I prefer the 27th, Wednesday. Of course this is the day before Thanksgiving, but I don't see how we can have it before that week. Do you think it would be convenient for your family to come down at that time. Write me immediately, if possible, what you think of this.

And then we have talked it over and think that a house wedding would be best at this time. Of course if things were different, I should like a Church wedding. but under the circumstances, it would hardly be the thing.

I think we can manage it very nicely though at the house.

The hour we have not decided on, whether at Five or Six P.M., but I think Six is perhaps better.

I presume you will select your "best man" and have that arranged.

I spoke to Mr. Parsell last week, and he wishes me to come at least part of this week, and then I say "Good Bye" to the place where I have spent so many happy hours.

Yesterday I sent in my resignation as Supt. of Primary Department to take effect next Sabbath. There is a certain sadness which we cannot shake off, when we turn from the paths that have been so pleasant, and give up the duties which have really been privileges and a joy to fulfill, but I suppose it will ever be so, each

changing scene will bring its
pleasures and sorrows, but when
we have put them together, we
shall find that they have "worked
out for us a far more exceeding
and eternal weight of glory."

And now I shall be so glad
when you come down and we can
talk matters over together. There
are many, many things to be
arranged yet, and I need your
opinion and assistance. On
Thursday night we have our C.
E. anniversary.

Well I must close. My love
to your mother. Sincerely
Abbie Rollin

Appendix 2: Howard's Poem to Abbie

1

forever
seeking
(helpless)

A homeless wanderer ~~by chance~~ I stray
Where Fate divine leads the way
Seeking, seeking but seeking
in vain.
For one the one her love to claim
That fond ideal of the heart
To call my own til death shall part
Full oft have I gazed at the throng
of earth
Drifting away on the stream
of mirth.
Methinks I at last have found
the one
The one I am to call my own
Visions of the future come
to my mind
At last the seeker has sought
to find.

2

These two lives that now are twain
Will blend in one & become
the same
By chance we meet O summers night
The pale orbed moon with
her silver light
Bathing the earth in a radiant silver sheen
Gives a loving charm to the
evening scene.
I see her in Fancy now as then
A poet's dream neer drawn by pen
Dreamy eyes of a liquid hue
Yet sparkling clear as the morning dew
Cheeks as fair as a cloud of summer
Tinged by the red a sunsets glimmer.
As the song is still heard though
the singer is gone
As the scene yet abides though
the train rushes on
As the melody lingers een after the playing
And the sunset remains though
darkness is straining

64

So still over those features so fair
Though seemingly sad a smile
lingered there
In a quiet retreat neath a fair
wooded bower
~~We sat & we talked of mind & its power~~
Intently I gazed as in magic power
& seen say you cannot thou reveal
The lot that is mine for woe or for weal
Taking her fair white hand in mine
Her fate I ~~then read~~ read line after line.
I see a life blest with years
A sad life mingled with hopes & fears
Of friends & lovers full many a score
A marriage fortunate could one wish for
more.
Yet clear & distinct I see there a
line
A line of deception her hand
trembles in mine

While seemingly true in life human
play
The part you enact for false is
your way.
Oh banish away these thoughts of thine
Tis not the truth false is the line."
"I read your fate just as I see it"
"You read yes but does truth decee it"
Her hand trembles & h can it be
This seemingly false is the truth
that I see.
The trembling tis past her hand she with draw
Like all wise decrees your presage has flaw
Some truth & some error but think
you to find
All truth & no error in these read-
ings of thine
Her last words burn deeply into
my heart.

Forgive I implore may true is your part
Though deeply we study the drama
of life
How often with error our study is rife
We judge we consider the parts
that each acts
Deducing false logic by misjudg-
ing the facts
The depth of any logic like the book
of the cover
War fair to the eye as far as the cover
For while the binding fine linen
for the page
Seek not within for treasures - only
dross to the sage
Fair in appearance, dear in
the cost
Seek within for treasures you
will find only dross.

For while I thus sought her
feelings to soothe
By a confession to error & so
on to prove
That perhaps now I had
failed in my reading
Having fallen in error forgiv-
ness was pleading
How shallow, how vain this
logic of mine -
While forgiveness imploring
Yet there was the line -
Be a sky of summer ever
so clear
Behind some hill a cloud
lurks near
Be the wandering moon ever
so bright
Some mage is awaiting, to shut out its light

Be your life now scattered along
with roses
On the crest of the morrow
Down deep in the heart some thorn
sorrow reposes
Be excuses so fair for engage-
ments were broken
Down deep in the heart are words
yet unspoken
Though forgiveness was granted given
for that fatal line.
The sorrow I had caused still
lurked in my mind
Though clouds conceal the sun
from the view
The day will soon come when the
sun will shine through
Though darkness obscure the pale
orbid light
There will soon come with a sky clear &
bright

Thus musing in silence the
minutes slipped by
Not caring to speak with down
cast eye
Seemingly seeing the ground
at my feet
But seeming to see for a face
fair & sweet
Would fain would arise before my
sight
A shadowy phantom of silvery
light
Ah twas my love of vanished
years
How often had those eyes
fused with tears
Pleadingly looked up in my own
while at her side I was
seated alone

9-

Pleadingly looked for slowly
silently day after day
Her life like a flower was
fading away
Fading passing away from
this life
Away from its sorrow away
from its strife
As a boat from its moorings
she sailed from life's shore
To eternity's ocean & her
life was no more.
In the cold silent earth
they laid her away
And with her my hopes were
buried for aye.
But why now on this evening night
Had this sad vision appeared
to my sight

10

~~But why now on this evening~~
~~night~~
~~Had this sad vision appeared~~
~~to my sight~~
The vision was gone I saw
but the ground
The silence unbroken save
the brook's moaning sound
~~And the softened whispers~~ ~~an~~
~~And the softened whispers of~~
~~the trees~~
~~the breeze~~ to read - by the on the
~~Lovely - sadly murmuring~~
~~the evening breeze -~~
~~to the trees~~
Arising I turned to bid her
adieu
Lovely - bewitching where the
moonlight broke through
A vision entrancing I gazed
without speaking
Was the seeker at last to
cease from his seeking
Had the music I love
that had slumbered so long

11

At last been awakened by
chords deep & strong
The hour tis late time runs
to waste -
Going so soon what need
I such haste
With a seen such as you
my evenings long
Stay but a moment for one
parting song
For I think thy spirit is
weary tonight
So stay but a moment &
under the light
Of the wandering moon &
the gleam I the star
To the music sweet I
a light guitar

She sang a song that
touched the heart
Of saddened lives though
now apart
Some days when weary
years have past
Each one will find its
own at last
The melody floated along
on the wind
At last the seeker would seek
to find
The cloud I despair was
sinking away.
The star I hope - Had it
risen for aye.

As if controlled by some strange power
In silence we sat unheeding the hour
Then arising to go I bade her farewell
Still held as it were in deep mystic spell
Oer head the stars bejewelled the sky
And large dark clouds now hurrying by
Would stay the beams of the pale orbed light
The air was laden with the strangeness of night
As if in a dream I wandered my way
Some echoing refrain still seeming to say
Some day when weary years have past
Each one will find its own again at last.

Printed in the United States
by Baker & Taylor Publisher Services